ME AND MY
FAMILY TREE

ME AND MY FAMILY TREE

by Joan Sweeney   illustrated by Annette Cable

SCHOLASTIC INC.

New York Toronto London Auckland Sydney
Mexico City New Delhi Hong Kong

Also by Joan Sweeney and Annette Cable
ME ON THE MAP
ME AND MY PLACE IN SPACE

For Patty, a very special branch of our family tree—J. S.

In memory of Alan—A. C.

ISBN 0-439-18466-5

Text copyright © 1999 by Joan Sweeney.
Illustrations copyright © 1999 by Annette Cable.
All rights reserved.
Published by Scholastic Inc., 555 Broadway, New York, NY 10012,
by arrangement with Random House Children's Books, a division of Random House, Inc.
SCHOLASTIC and associated logos are trademarks and/or registered
trademarks of Scholastic Inc.

12 11 10 9 8 7 6 5 4 3 2 1   0 1 2 3 4 5/0

Printed in the U.S.A.   09

First Scholastic printing, September 2000

This is me and my family.

I have a brother, a mommy and a daddy, grandparents,
aunts and uncles, and cousins too.
How are they all related to me?
I'll show you on my family tree.

First I start with me.

Then comes my big brother, Alan.

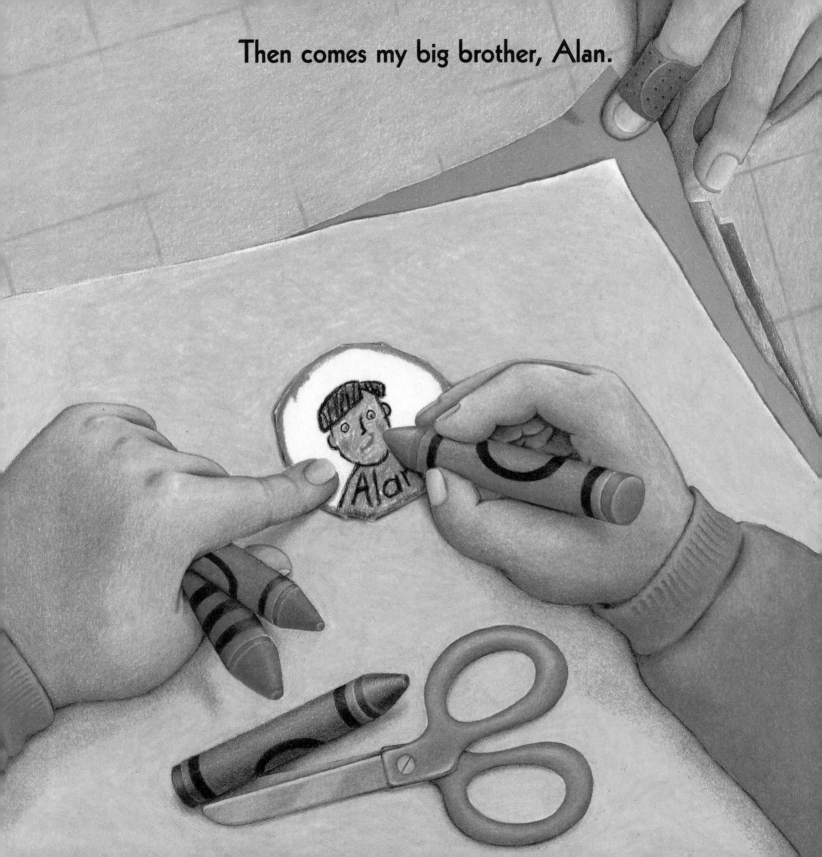

We're both part of my family tree.

These are my parents—
my mommy and daddy.

They're part of my family tree.

This is my mommy's
mommy—my grandma.

This is my mommy's
daddy—my grandpa.

This is my daddy's
mommy—my nana.

This is my daddy's
daddy—my poppa.

They're all part of my family tree.

Mommy has a sister—my Aunt Sally. She's married to my
Uncle Lee. They have a daughter—my cousin Alice.

They're all part of my family tree.

Daddy has a brother—my Uncle Jim. He's married to my Aunt Margie. They have two sons—my cousin Jeff and my cousin David. Daddy also has a sister—that's my Aunt Pat.

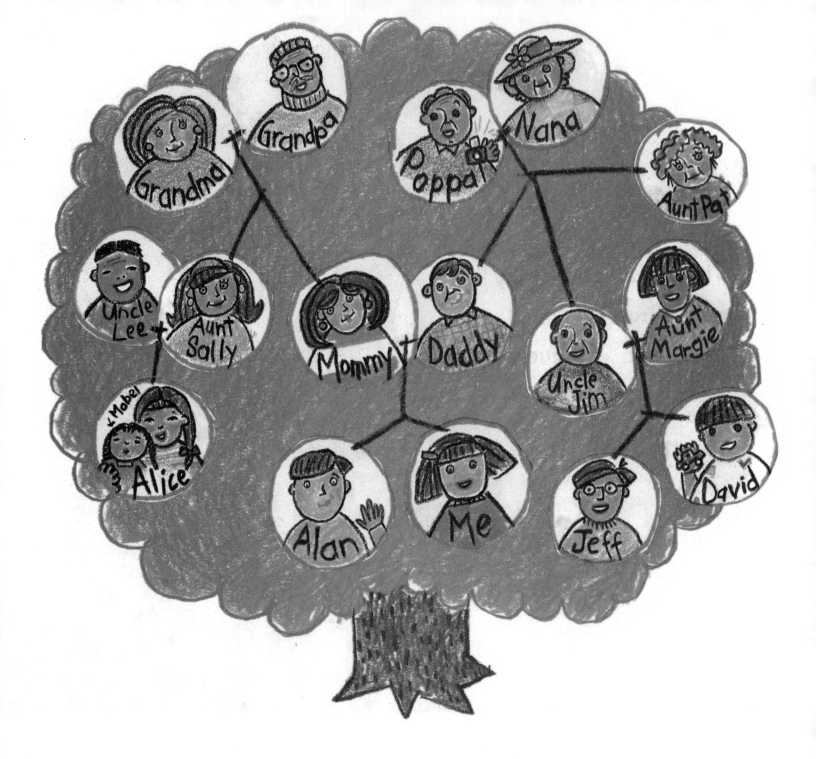

They're *all* part of my
family tree.
Now—can you guess how
I came to be?

Grandma and Grandpa had Mommy and her sister.

Nana and Poppa had Daddy and his brother and sister.

My aunts and uncles
had my cousins.

Mommy and Daddy
had my brother.

And then . . . Mommy and Daddy had *me!*

One day I may have children, and
they'll be part of my family tree.

Think of it! Everyone in the world has a family tree.

Just like you and me.

My Family

Grandma & Grandpa

Grandma & Grandpa

aunts & uncles

aunts & uncles

Mommy

Daddy

cousins

cousins

brothers

me

sisters